Date: 9/18/15

J 796.33264 MIA
Zappa, Marcia,
Miami Dolphins /

The NFL's Greatest Teams

MIAMI DOLPHINS

Dolphins

17

Big Buddy Books
An Imprint of Abdo Publishing
www.abdopublishing.com

Marcia Zappa

www.abdopublishing.com

Published by Abdo Publishing, a division of ABDO, PO Box 398166, Minneapolis, Minnesota 55439.
Copyright © 2015 by Abdo Consulting Group, Inc. International copyrights reserved in all countries. No part
of this book may be reproduced in any form without written permission from the publisher. Big Buddy Books™
is a trademark and logo of Abdo Publishing.

Printed in the United States of America, North Mankato, Minnesota.
042014
092014

Cover Photo: ASSOCIATED PRESS.
Interior Photos: ASSOCIATED PRESS.

Coordinating Series Editor: Rochelle Baltzer
Contributing Editors: Bridget O'Brien, Sarah Tieck
Graphic Design: Michelle Labatt

Library of Congress Cataloging-in-Publication Data

Zappa, Marcia, 1985-
  Miami Dolphins / Marcia Zappa.
     pages cm. -- (The NFL's greatest teams)
  ISBN 978-1-62403-362-9
1. Miami Dolphins (Football team)--History--Juvenile literature. I. Title.
  GV956.M47Z37 2015
  796.332'640975938--dc23
                        2013051240

Contents

A Winning Team

Gearing Up

Aqua green, orange, blue, and white are the team's colors.

   The Miami Dolphins are a football team from Miami, Florida. They have played in the National Football League (NFL) for more than 40 years.

   The Dolphins have had good seasons and bad. But time and again, they've proven themselves. Let's see what makes the Dolphins one of the NFL's greatest teams.

The Dolphins are the only NFL team to win every game in an entire season and postseason!

League Play

Team Standings

The AFC and the National Football Conference (NFC) make up the NFL. Each conference has a north, south, east, and west division.

The NFL got its start in 1920. Its teams have changed over the years. Today, there are 32 teams. These teams make up two conferences and eight divisions.

The Dolphins play in the East Division of the American Football Conference (AFC). This division also includes the Buffalo Bills, the New England Patriots, and the New York Jets.

The Bills (*above*), the Jets, and the Patriots are all rivals of the Dolphins.

Kicking Off

The Miami Dolphins became a team in 1966. The team was founded by Joseph Robbie and Danny Thomas.

Like many new teams, the Dolphins struggled at first. Coach Don Shula turned the team around. In 1972, the team made it to their first Super Bowl. Sadly, they lost to the Dallas Cowboys 24–3.

Time Out

The Dolphins' owners held a contest to pick the team's name. More than 1,000 different names were suggested!

Before joining the Dolphins, Shula was the head coach for the Baltimore Colts. Between the two teams, he has more wins than any other NFL coach!

Highlight Reel

Win or Go Home

NFL teams play 16 regular season games each year. The teams with the best records are part of the play-off games. Play-off winners move on to the conference championship. Then, conference winners face off in the Super Bowl!

The next season, the Dolphins came back strong. They won all of their games! They went on to the 1973 Super Bowl. They beat the Washington Redskins 14–7. They are the only team to win the Super Bowl with a perfect regular season!

The Dolphins returned to the Super Bowl in 1974. They beat the Minnesota Vikings 24–7. The team stayed strong. But they didn't make it to another Super Bowl until 1983. They lost to the Washington Redskins 27–17.

In 1974, the Dolphins became the first NFL team to play in the Super Bowl three years in a row.

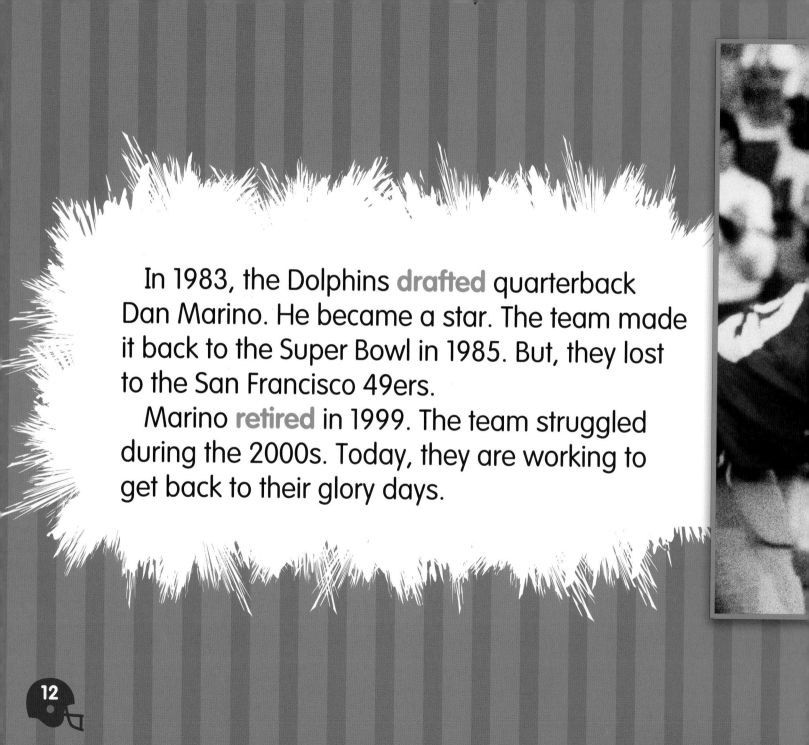

In 1983, the Dolphins **drafted** quarterback Dan Marino. He became a star. The team made it back to the Super Bowl in 1985. But, they lost to the San Francisco 49ers.

Marino **retired** in 1999. The team struggled during the 2000s. Today, they are working to get back to their glory days.

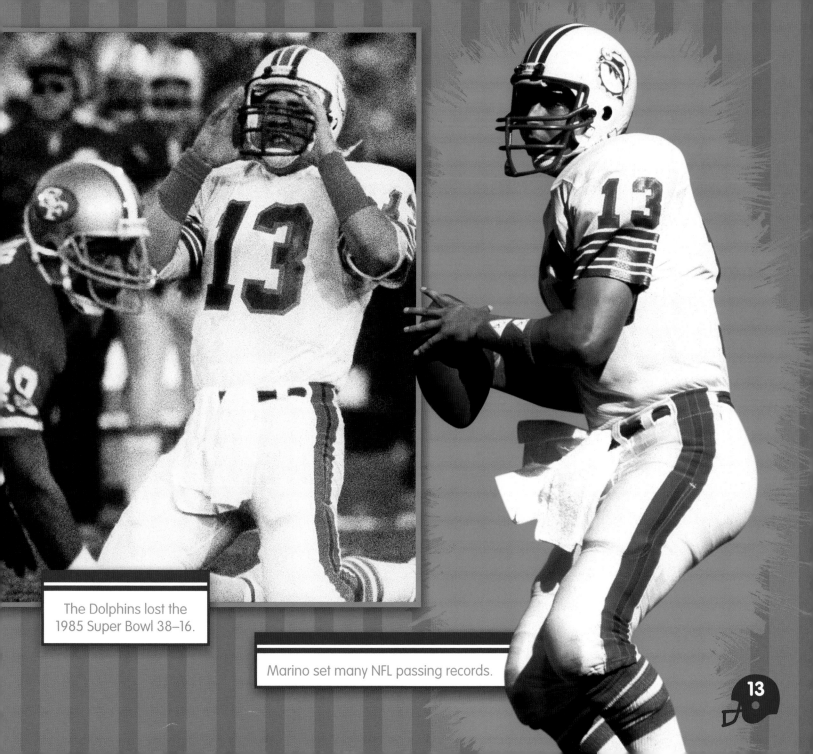

The Dolphins lost the
1985 Super Bowl 38–16.

Marino set many NFL passing records.

13

Halftime! Stat Break

Team Records

RUSHING YARDS
Career: Larry Csonka, 6,737 yards (1968–1974, 1979)
Single Season: Ricky Williams, 1,853 yards (2002)
PASSING YARDS
Career: Dan Marino, 61,361 yards (1983–1999)
Single Season: Dan Marino, 5,084 yards (1984)
RECEPTIONS
Career: Mark Clayton, 550 receptions (1983–1992)
Single Season: O.J. McDuffie, 90 receptions (1998)
ALL-TIME LEADING SCORER
Olindo Mare, 1,048 points (1997–2006)

Famous Coaches

Don Shula (1970–1995)

Championships

SUPER BOWL APPEARANCES:
1972, 1973, 1974, 1983, 1985

SUPER BOWL WINS:
1973, 1974

Pro Football Hall of Famers & Their Years with the Dolphins

Nick Buoniconti, Linebacker (1969–1974, 1976)
Larry Csonka, Fullback (1968–1974, 1979)
Bob Griese, Quarterback (1967–1980)
Jim Langer, Center (1970–1979)
Larry Little, Guard (1969–1980)

Dan Marino, Quarterback (1983–1999)
Don Shula, Coach (1970–1995)
Dwight Stephenson, Center (1980–1987)
Paul Warfield, Wide Receiver (1970–1974)

Fan Fun

NICKNAMES: The Fins, The Fish
STADIUM: Sun Life Stadium
LOCATION: Miami Gardens, Florida
MASCOT: T.D.

Coaches' Corner

In 1970, Don Shula took over the Dolphins as head coach. He spent 26 years with the team. During this time, they only had two losing seasons! They appeared in five Super Bowls and won two of them.

Shula led the Dolphins to 274 wins.

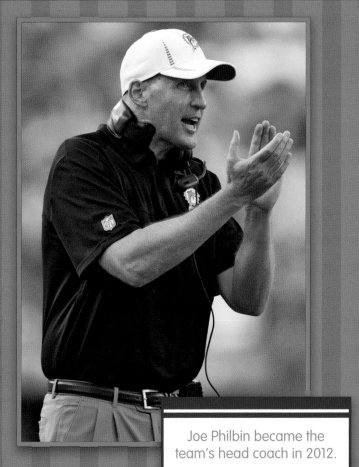

Joe Philbin became the team's head coach in 2012.

Star Players

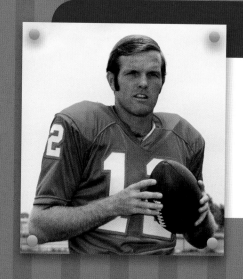

Bob Griese QUARTERBACK (1967–1980)

The Dolphins **drafted** Bob Griese as their first pick in 1967. He led the team to nine winning seasons during the 1970s. This included three Super Bowl appearances and two wins. Griese was known for his **accurate** passing.

Larry Csonka FULLBACK (1968–1974, 1979)

Larry Csonka was a powerful fullback. He helped the team reach the Super Bowl three times in a row. In the 1974 Super Bowl, he was named the Most Valuable Player (MVP).

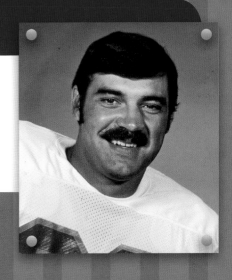

Larry Little GUARD (1969–1980)

Larry Little was an important part of the team's strong rushing game in the 1970s. Little played in the Pro Bowl, which is the NFL's all-star game, five times. And, he was the AFC's Lineman of the Year three times.

Jake Scott SAFETY (1970–1975)

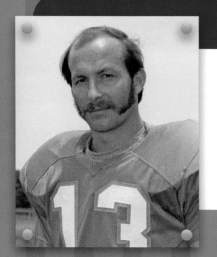

Jake Scott was a leader of the team's "No-Name Defense." They were called that because they weren't often talked about. But, they were very important. Scott helped the Dolphins have a perfect season in 1972. And, he was named the 1973 Super Bowl's MVP.

Dan Marino QUARTERBACK (1983–1999)

Dan Marino became the team's starting quarterback in 1983. The next year, he became the NFL's MVP. Marino became the NFL's leading passer in 1995. By the time he **retired**, he had broken many NFL passing records.

Zach Thomas LINEBACKER (1996–2007)

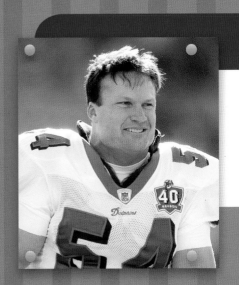

Zach Thomas played for the Dolphins for 12 seasons. He had more than 1,600 tackles. He also had 17 **interceptions** and four touchdowns! Thomas was selected to play in the Pro Bowl seven times.

Jason Taylor DEFENSIVE END/LINEBACKER (1997–2007, 2009, 2011)

Jason Taylor was a powerful defensive player for the Dolphins. During his **career**, he had more than 130 sacks. Only five NFL players have had more. In 2006, he was named the NFL's Defensive Player of the Year.

Sun Life Stadium

The Dolphins play home games at Sun Life Stadium. It is in a **suburb** of Miami called Miami Gardens. Sun Life Stadium opened in 1987. It was redone in 2007. It can hold about 75,500 people.

Sun Life Stadium has hosted the Super Bowl five times. The most recent time was in 2010.

23

Fins Fans

Thousands of fans flock to Sun Life Stadium to see the Dolphins play home games. In 1997, the team got a new **mascot**. T.D. is a dolphin that is seven feet (2 m) tall. He wears a football uniform and helmet. T.D. appears at home games. He helps fans cheer on their team.

Some Dolphins fans call their team "the Fins" or "the Fish."

T.D. stands for "the Dolphin."

Final Call

The Miami Dolphins have a long, rich history. They were a force in the NFL soon after becoming a team in 1966. In 1972, they became the only NFL team to have a perfect season.

Recent years have been less successful. But, true fans have stuck with them. Many believe that the Miami Dolphins will remain one of the NFL's greatest teams.

The 1972 Dolphins are remembered as one of the all-time greatest teams. Coach Shula (*right*) and his players are still honored today.

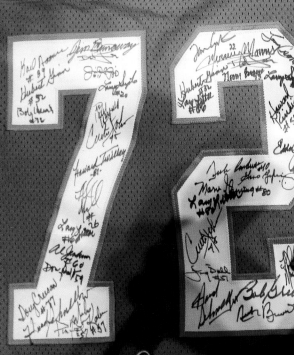

Through the Years

1970

Don Shula becomes the head coach. The team has its first winning season.

1983

Paul Warfield becomes the first Dolphin in the Pro Football Hall of Fame.

1972

The Dolphins play in their first Super Bowl.

1974

The Dolphins play in their third Super Bowl in a row. This sets an NFL record.

1966

The Dolphins become a **professional** football team.

1973

The team wins the Super Bowl. This finishes its perfect 1972 season.

1995

Dan Marino breaks the NFL's **career** passing yards record!

2013

The team gets a new logo.

1987

Joe Robbie Stadium opens. Later, it is renamed Sun Life Stadium.

2010

The Super Bowl is played at Sun Life Stadium. It is the fifth time it has been held there. And, it is the tenth time it's been in Miami.

1997

T.D. becomes the team's **mascot**.

Postgame Recap

1. Who became the NFL's career passing yards leader in 1995?
   A. Bob Griese   **B**. Don Shula   **C**. Dan Marino

2. What major NFL record did the Dolphins set during the 1972 season?
   A. The most points scored during a season
   B. The first entirely undefeated and untied season
   C. The fewest touchdowns allowed during a season

3. Name 3 of the 9 Dolphins in the Pro Football Hall of Fame.

4. Which of these teams is a rival of the Dolphins?
   A. The Buffalo Bills
   B. The Seattle Seahawks
   C. The Chicago Bears

Glossary

accurate free from mistakes.

career work a person does to earn money for living.

draft a system for professional sports teams to choose new players. When a team drafts a player, they choose that player for their team.

interception (ihn-tuhr-SEHP-shuhn) when a player catches a pass that was meant for the other team's player.

mascot something to bring good luck and help cheer on a team.

professional (pruh-FEHSH-nuhl) working for money rather than only for pleasure.

retire to give up one's job.

suburb a town, village, or community just outside a city.

Websites

To learn more about the NFL's Greatest Teams, visit **booklinks.abdopublishing.com**. These links are routinely monitored and updated to provide the most current information available.

Index